THIR13EN

LETTERS FROM EXILE

CAROLINA

For the person who was the source of inspiration for my poems.

Yes, you need a reason to write.

Contents

Contents

Contents

Foreword

Writing is a creative form of recreation; it not only stops the past from holding the person hostage but also gives different perspectives to life. The way a person grooms and dresses create a personal style of the physical self. Similarly, the way a person pens down her thoughts, chooses words and structures the sentences describes her literary style and her heart.

This book titled, "Thirteen" is not just a youngster's fairy tale; it exhibits the talent and personality of the author expressing herself through the written word. I enjoyed reading through her collection of her poems, and in the process, I discovered her ideas on the beauty of nature, life experiences and imaginations echoing through the pages. She has deconstructed her complex emotions into simple text in the form of epigrammatic poems.

I would like to appreciate Ms. Carolina Salomi for her wise initiative of publishing a book. I am sure her parents and well wishers would have been a strong pillar of support for such a worthwhile cause. I wish the poems in this book would bring sweet memories to all the readers and carry them to a world of artistic reality with a personal connect.

As her proud teacher, and as the Head, Department of Physics, Women's Christian College, where Ms. Carolina Salome is presently doing her undergraduate degree, I consider it a privilege to write this foreword for her first book titled, "Thirteen" She has proved that literature is a form of art used as a tool to communicate one's thoughts, feelings, experiences and opinions irrespective of the academic background or specialization.

I wish her success in all her academic endeavours and a blessed future.

Dr. A. Christina Nancy

June 2022

Preface

These poems deal with the myriad experiences and the ordeals of a teenage girl living in a bustling metropolitan city in a South Asian country. While some of the poems in this collection are based on my lived experiences, others are inspired by the stories that I have heard and the sagas that I have been exposed to over a period of time. The poems in this anthology intend to offer the reader a window into the world of an Indian teenager, the rollercoaster of emotions that come with it, and what it is to be a teenager navigating the challenges of living through a global pandemic, studies, relationships, and life in general in a third world country. The poems are at once both personal and fictive, effectively combining the power of imagination to convey slices of life. The poems are written in a lucid language with an intention to establish a personal connect with the readers. Initially, the poems in this collection were not written with the intention to be compiled into an anthology ; they were written at different instances and in different points of time in my life. The idea behind compiling them into such an anthology is to chronicle my everyday experiences in print form for the sake of posterity. It is a means for me to make sense of my jigsaw-puzzle like thoughts and put them into a tangible, coherent whole. They are in a sense, a pathway for my emotions to find creative expression through the medium of the written word. - Carolina

Acknowledgements

Firstly, I would like to thank the Almighty for the ability to do this work and for everything He gave me. I thank all my friends and my family who supported me.

I would like to acknowledge the extraordinary dept I owe to my respected teacher Dr. Christina Nancy who whole heartedly supported and encouraged me to complete this anthology. I am greatful for the support , encouragement, sincere guidance of my teachers Ms. Angelin Premkumari and Mr. Paul Israel for helping me bring out my poems in the form of an anthology. I also thank Women's Christian College and Physics department for the support and help.

I would like to express my special thanks to my brother Jeffrey Gabriel and my friends Jenefa Angelin, Rithvika, Leean Sreeja, Anunshia Ruth for their constant source of love, support and for their comments which encouraged me.

I thank Notion Press publication and I also extent my heartfelt thanks to all my well wishers.

1. THE LIGHT FOUNDED THE DARK

The incongruity flame flickers with no hope and clue
Fighting to retain the spark to be found in the dark
Flourishing with leaves but with no goodness and smile
Canopy of branches waving for one more chance of life
Bare feet ; forbidden soul under the smite of sun
Almost stoned with all bruises while left on the ground
The eyes of love noticed the unworthy vessel left astray
Moulded it into a fine sculpture and engraved on the holy hands
Covered, rescued and accepted the darkness to shine on me.

2. SHE WAS IN LOVE

All is now a wish to visit the cold stars with pure heart to fall in love
With white shiny blameless dress on and the tiny tears embedded on it
The eyes of her embellished with innocence to talk with the song of wind
The mirror on the sky longing to be noticed by the pleasing look of her
A pale shimmer of moon light kissed her cheek to admire sculpted diamond
The words has numbed her body to rise and appreciate the forlorn night
Lovely euphony amidst the blurry mist tore the air to call her
Paved a romantic way with the love burning on the lampstand
Her hand carried her pride of roses and bravery in her for herself in her heart
Flower waved at her with happy tears to experience the truthfulness of love
She broke the glasses with her delicate hand to hold the pride of her smile
The soft bare legs ran fast splashing the waters on the way

The light on the sky groomed her with a crown of contentment of love

She started dancing to the rhythm of rain and to the beat of her heart.

3. BEAVERED SMILE

Guitar embraced my heart and my fingers hugging my pen with selfish
To breath the fragrance of the lament with a summon of little relief
A bright rose on the ground rose from the frozen land with pierced wound
Shakes its head looking at my eyes, singing the elegies to the old me with sound
Do you remember all my poem of smile written on water waves to stay
Bringing it all to the finest picture to decorate my eouligies with clay
I'm not sure from where it had all started to conclude with a hint
The pages of inconsequential book was worn out flying along with the wind.

4. THE BEAT OF THE RAIN

The passionate heart in the arcade seeks the rain beat
Now the cold breeze and rain drop has reached her eyes
The perfect song is blinding all the spot light to shine
Because all the gleam is ruined by the light of our smile
The rhythm of ours is syncing exceptionally well in the rain
All the tears of pain is wiped by the wet hand to claim
These dark clouds above has move the dark clouds behind
Shouting at top of lungs and the brightest laughter to begun
The frozen smile and fixed heart in the winter has melted
By all the drops of happiness from the sky is growing faster
The icy cold night numbing all the tears of happiness on me
Singing the lyrics of my dust filled book to glow is all I see
The wind is blowing all the pages at the midnight and everytime
When I dance in the rain with myself to seek the mystery of all time.

5. AUTUMN AMBIGUITY

Small little shine on the face and the sweet smell of twilight
Bare foot on the cloistered pathway, a step forward to feel the bleeding
Flaws are hidden under the dark clouds for the dwindle decisions
They are the same when idle moon has reached the heart of none
Rain drop on my cheeks wondering where it is from
Saying it is all above the sky and reality of life
Calm cold breeze brushing my hair, whispering solitary
And I heard a loudest voice of the moist silence of mine.

6. OBLIVION PETRICHOR

Small little shine on the face and the sweet smell of twilight
Bare foot on the cloistered pathway, a step forward to feel the bleeding
Flaws are hidden under the dark clouds for the dwindle decisions
They are the same when idle moon has reached the heart of none
Rain drop on my cheeks wondering where it is from
Saying it is all above the sky and reality of life
Calm cold breeze brushing my hair whispering solitary
And I heard a loudest voice of the moist silence of mine.

7. THE SPECIAL

An aesthetic door way led to a big hall
To the dark room which had no people at all
The great books were arranged all over
On a old rugged book holder
The light from the window glared at the book
It had such an ordinary appearance
Was not much greater than all other roses
The blanket of the book was not smooth as snow
Not with the capturing chapters to glow
Left astray, not literally; but it doesn't know
It was not much fascinating to read
But the caring finger picked the book
The light glared at the eyes from its gap
The cover was dusted and the hinge was shined
"The Special Sorry" Was engraved on the cover
It was not much bold or talented
But the title was admired and made forced to open
It was adorned with a adorable heart
Numerous chapters was gracefully read
Even it was not touched by others
It was hugged close to the chest
It was considered special for its words

Now each and every venomous hand pulled
Not to read but to ruin the pages
Now the challenging chapters went through an ordeal
The story was not pleasing to the lovable eyes
Those chapters disappointed the smile
The warmth feeling was gone and left alone
The wind flipped all the pages
Now it could feel the dust on its face
It waited for the hands to be lifted
The book was expected to give the first move
But it was waiting for the perfect time to show
The book of thorns was expected to bloom into roses
Waiting for it to say the title again to heal all the bruises

8. HYSTERICAL HORIZON

Silhouette on the moon, singing the fantasy
I know the truth and the perfect pages for me
Saw the white rose twinkling amidst the eventide
At the far end of my misty blurry vision I see
It gleamed inside my eyes with a pause on me;
My feet moved a step forward gently to see
Wanting it to touch was like a hysterical horizon
Which is beautiful; but it is too far to reach the height
Here the heart beats like an echo around me
And it fades into a exquisite brilliant melody.
But I don't like all the blush made by the ocean
And I almost levitated above the clear waves.

9. UNDER THE SAME SKY

Two little souls under the different pattern of sky
But all the same stars are smiling at the night
Wouldn't want to say all the smiles or frowns
All I know was it will stay at the very most end
Never experienced the gladness of twilight care
Holding on even at all my silliest act of love
All the action are not expressive but a laconic
To say it all in a simple sentence of good heart
Staying at even at the worst part of the sky
Privileged to have a beautiful bond of brother
Don't really missing all the light at the night sky
It is really you who made me strong amidst the lie.

10. WIND OF EPIPHANY

Holding the fewest fear and love on either side of reality
Driving on a lone highway with the light of moon simplicity
The music beat drops when there is a pause on the cloistered way
The voices of laconic echoing all the way while wanting to stay;
This is a ridiculous reason to know the truth of the cheers in the heart
Saving the love like night sky to shine brighter at the day dream part
The head lights blinding the way of other direction on the longest way
The wind from the windows was not strong as the music in mind that crave
Faster than flashback and cooler than eyes on the non stop vibe
Seeing the walls of muse, at the end of the road with little soul alive.

11. SCARLET LETTER

A new silence at the background telling that is all
Pretending as simple paper on a old vintage table
Perturbed petals falling along the prose of lament snow
With all ink of muse inside a salient sophisticated pen
On the ragged paper with the stories of a fixed heart
Writing, "Yeah this is same old weather all around"
Holding a delicate glass close to chest with care
And you could read every blank words on my eyes
Wondering it's staying in even a calamitous fragile land
You said "To fade away I'm not a season, you're the reason"
Now the fingers armed with love, trembles with suspicious glare
And the heart beats with question to whom these words belong
All the praying petals has reached down the table of disability
The letter is crushed, left behind the broken pieces of glass on the floor.

12. RENDEZVOUS SERINDIPITY

Rouge star appeared amidst the dark stygian rainy day
Carried a melody behind which is my plangent to express
Tears of fondness of you in my heart rendered when it entered;
The zephyr froze my mind to stay at present
Before you know I was gasping for breath
The aurora is refulgent in the sky after these many years
All the afterglow are not gonna evanescent easily as you think
My heart stayed even after the namesake farewell
Ethereal symphony played at the silent background
With the misty eyes and a cherubic quavering heart
Seemed like a ridiculous plot of fragile fantasy book
Not expecting the propitious denouement complication.

13. SMILE OF THE GLITTERS

Just imagining all the desire of clue less heart
Standing alone in a crowd which is never sought
Everything sounds too much because it's hard to claim
Sometimes all the smiles roll down as repenting rain
Thinking that it's made of every famed flaws of feathers
Leaning on a invisible shoulder preparing for another
I can hear all the voices of a silent smile dreaming
And all the aching peaceful elegant eyes quarreling
Each and every glitters from heart is shining
Hoping for the best of thine to hold the rain

14. THE GOLD DUST

I'm not the priority I'm not on the list
To see the how it looks or feel
I'm just unpretentious empty vase on the corner
Where there is no greater light to notice
Which don't deserve a decorated flowers
To make it attractive or to adorned
Same old stories and exaggeration echoes
Made it feel heavier and lost alone
Was broken every single time to hurt
The gold dust flies every time it fells
It fixed and healed at all fallings
And glowed to arise stronger than ever
Shinned at the darkness of others
Now it own nothing to lose in this world
That made it so much happier.

15. THE BEAT OF YOU

The sun is shining on a cold morning busy road
The wind is vibing along with the beat of my dance
And there where all the eyes looked up and down
My music of you muted all the noise of the world
I don't want only the best but also the complication of you
Being the bright light on the daylight singing with me the new
All the billion smile on my eyes gleaming like never before
It is just the happiest heart in the whole world is dancing
Knowing that it's the perfect sky for the blue ocean
Singing with the beauty of flaws with my whole heart.

16. ALBUM OF MUSE

They say time flies but it has frozen like a photograph
Every picture is crossing in front of my eyes of muse
Lost in the secret silent leaning on the wall thinking it was new
Mind of music is slowly blooming and wind on my cheeks
Kissing the love of nostalgia which was written on the paper
The sun touched my eyes in the dark scented room of you
Every piece of mirror on the floor reflecting your ocean eyes
Looking at me smiling the memories and which will go on
And every time all voices around turned it into ashes
Thinking its not worth and lost but my heart is phoenix
Always waiting at the distance admiring how my rose is in the glass
I won't touch; afraid that the flame on my hand would hurt it.

17. SPRING AT WINTER NIGHT

A strong brave rock standing with mighty look
Lost the hope of love on which it was leaning
But majestic cover never stumbled or moved
There was ache inside the bold look of smile
The reminding rain poured down like a fall
Showed the gleam of moon on her cheek
The rock bloomed and realized the gain of hope
There was shining spring amidst the winter night.

18. HANDPRINTS ON THE HEART

You got to stop all the nice lies of mind's art
I think no one can know the lightness in my heart
When it is surrounded by with all hype of music
Shooting stars are lighting up the sky of basic
It is skipping a heartbeat with impression of star
The soul is levitating among the clouds so far
Holding mesmerizing sparks on the right of light
And majestic melody on the other side of fight
Just the dancing with the wind being itself
Doesn't care even when the sun sets with a laugh.

19. THE VISION OF BLIND EYES

A lot of complications on the simplest pale sky
It had lost in the harmony of wind floating on my hands
Placed my bare foot on lose sand with a hope of care
The small love of breeze made me feel my heart and bones
Stars starring the gleam of eyes of untold stories
Which was flowing like a stream of river and ending at the ocean
The waves just touched the toes of unrealistic hope
But it had overwhelmed the hopeless heavy heart
It is beating like the birds flattering it's wings to reach the sunset
Going far to reach its home to achieve it's aching desire
The ocean hid another moon safe inside with its hug of horizon
Each water whispering the wonderful tale to its own light
The wondering hand touched the clouds with eyes of hope
It held so tight with a mesmerizing view of sad painting
That one zephyr pulled my eyes to close like moon did waves
It viewed a billion beautiful art harmonizing in front of my soul
I saw all the stories on her face which I said all night
There where I realized to turn blind to see what I love.

20. ENCHANTING ENIGMA

I saw myself standing with a rose with its head down
Singing the poetry from the heart which was never shown
Following the footprints on the barren land leading to place I never known
Picking the crushed paper of night from the ground with a tear of grown
Moving with the view of double vision seeing all with light of love
But feet running with a fight, passing every shadow of tree's bow
There was moment where the pace was paused with a aching roar
Like the butterflies in my heart has left the home of my shore
Lost its way, cloistered among the rustling whispering to give up
The hill with the gleaming peak got her attention of her soul
Poised feet resumed her run to reach the shine and to see the dusk
It was too late and those letter on her hand is not of worth of that land
Her bleeding hands planted the rose and decorated with the tears
She walked towards the sunset, blurry vision admiring stars
But her butterflies rested on the rose, it beat like her heart did

They never left, because it always felt like home.

21. WISTORAGIC WREATH

I know that you know the questions for my letters
But it's all buried deep inside everytime and letting it to grow
I don't want the broken pieces of glasses to be a vase
So I'm letting my heart to fly among the clouds and pour down as rain
With a breeze of muse on the bleeding hands to heal
Leaving everything behind carrying the blurry view with the answers
Do you remember the line which didn't suit me at all
Is this the place did stairs of "it'll go" led me to?

22. THE NIGHT AFTER THE DAY

They were the beautiful days before night
Now my memories always chase and fight
My expectations are always greater than my expressions
Well my frowns are from my frustation
A new character was added to the story
It has exacerbated the bright sad story
There's diffrence between realise and understand
In my case they both always stand
Thought that the thoughts were synced
Finally te eyes were blinked.

23. INEFFABLE

I'm not so good at reading the letter of my soul
So the broken pieces of paper heart want to write
Heart beat is pacing but hands a couldn't cope with it
Wondering hands not knowing why it can't feel
As the eyes were showing what words couldn't
There's so many blank pages on the book
Wanting to paint an art with words and letting go
But no book was closed before the beginning
The tears of poetry wrote everything and was ready to fly
But I know it's holding on like the starts in the sky of muse

24. FIRST EVER HEART BEAT

Seeing you was not a well planned plot of a story
But something happened when I reached the scene
May not be the movie fantasy with stars and roses
But I saw the whole world infront of my misery eyes
Never knew how it feels gaze stars from the sky
Until I saw my future blazes in your smile
Nothing can replace the lyrics which always shows you
All the time of my days played the song of you heart beat
Written with the silent touch of your love on my cheeks
Someday I'll hold your hand as I held you in my heart.

25. ARMED WITH SOLITARY

Brightest colours of the day dream sky of cheers
But it never been the light which stay on the night
Created an echo of laugh when all where lost to view
When I wandered in the oblivion of smite of sun
I jumped from the sky armed with scented solitary
Spreading the wings with the fragrance of love
Clearing the dew blowing my hair when I'm flying down
Barely seeing the ground with invisible snow
Those dew near my eyes flew far high to the clouds
Holding on the way was like clinging on for what I need
The transparent wind trying to hide the sun shine
So as it goes when try to stop the pace of fewest
The catastrophe heart leading the bruised beat
Still the roses never failed to knew the blushes
The rhyming rhythm of it is not easy to love
Which is so complicated with sophisticated night
Searching the fading flim scene of thirteen.

26. DELIPHATIC DAYDREAM

The sword with a mystery edge with a misery handle
Writes it's heart with a essence of eulogies
Every mouth lip synced to the cruel summer
Nobody knows the stories after the thin line, at the end of each poems.
Thoughts on the air creeping inside the roots of my mind
Without leaving a scar on the hands it escapes
Standing still like a solitary tree inside a factory
Nobody can understand these seasons of all the sentence.
Making it to regret even after the giving the best
Not blaming the time, maybe its all reflection of mine
But I've never saw the December cold on my mirror
No, nobody can see the flashback of this wounded feathers.

27. ELYSIAN EXIT

Those tiny little flowers welcoming the unsolicited
Still this foolish heart never got those lines
Saw all those decorated table with roses and white linen
Seemed like a familiar story of a sad end loving author
Holding a skeptic glass of fine wine
But it was never ever better than you
And I saw you walking along the aisle gleaming
All of sudden the camera flashed at my eyes
But it brought the whole story in a single second
I promise I smiled with my whole heart there
While my mind and heart having a conversation
My eyes looked at your creating your poetry
As my credulous clock was ticking, I left.

28. DELICATE CRIME

Why the sun is filling the room while the dusk is calling stars?
Why all the lavenders are white when you're gleaming in my eyes?
Maybe it's my barren branches blooming your view
Now every words is running like a stream with no clue
Would you like to see my delicate dreams in the sky
And I'm blaming myself for the innocent delinquent act of yours
Breaking the guards with a majestic walk on the hallway
All the footprint are still alive in the heart giving the hint in the crime.

29. EPIC EPILOUGE

Keys of black and white lied to all the time
So I took ride to the peak of perishing light
The leaves responded to every step of my walk
Rustling all the way of my pageant look
But I wanted to move in simple silence of reality
Flaws on the bark of the tree embracing the whole land
Reminding the reflection on the water gleaming white
My letters sailed to mystery end as paper boats
The light started to give a glitch between the leaves
Waving at them while they were almost to drown
Pacing heart beat made it to reach the paradise
But a million letters scattered at the boundary
And now the piano played the right epilogue to the story book.

30. MISERY AND BRAVERY

Veins on my hands could feel winter glitters
The gold crown failed to shine in front of the majestic walk
All the paths taking me to the place of my royalty high
You armed with roses and those powerful glare on the eyes
No glitch on the view was like a perfectly sculpted sculpture
Horses of bravery and misery either side of me
Cuff on my wrist dragged me behind the golden bars
For breaking the doors of heart and blaming the king.
Now everything stealing the breath in my lungs
And sending them to stars to conquer the palace
But the sun tore my skin and my eyes burning
Buried my sword of victory under the tree
Writing your name in the prison wall of wonder
Wondering what's behind the shining flame and burning attitude?

31. I LOST

The time has lost its patience for this trivial soul
Heard all my imperfect heart beats calling to be mine
Not much sophisticated as it is in my head
But my heart lingering in the yards of pleasant smile
The fragrance all over my body is following me
Chasing the imaginary butterflies with unrealistic wings
Now all the voices echoing all the way "you ruined it"
It was never new so I moved but with a scar
Each and every ecstatic story are not embraced as it seems
It's holding a elougie and raising from the grave for the sake
Just to know the story from your side and go back again
As my letters are not clear like glass to rain down to you
And I never thought they'll flow endless but without clue
Wishing that I had a chance to say what I have to confess to the sky
Afraid that it might refuse to shine and understand
As the ocean depths is not known unless you drown
Looking back the time where I failed to remember the pain
But now the gun shot straight to my heart giving permanent scar
Realizing that time is tricky and changing every second.
Building a bridge to destroy and to drown in the sea
Someday I'll leave the field when she comes to take care

Your picture, my reflection ; smile on my eyes

32. EMPTY SPACE

Cold glass covering around me without a space to breath
Looking for my face in the happiest crowd from heaven and beneath
So I guess I'll spend my life with the empty space of solitary
Preparing to face nothing because the sword is out my hand
My hands is freezing, and my face is numbing to it's cruelty
And my mirror is giving a crack after the reflection of mine,
Papers are flying to help themselves from the stories I write
Wondering how I didn't run to escape and take a refuge
Lips eulogize me for every speech but turns blind to see the depths
And destroyed with simple words and now I lost my way
Hoping that the air rescue me before I'm out of my breath
As it is almost closing to satisfy it's long term wish.

33. FALICITATE WALK

The jacket is flying to the wind creating catastrophe
To all the heart with raising the pace inside the ribs
The beat dropped down when he crossed me
And sowed a rose of unexpected serendipity
My mind in the brood woods after knowing the fact
But the face is not fading from the sky, even after the storm
Every mellifluous chirping between the leaves echoing
My feet gradually moving towards the crackers light at twilight
Main character in the flim scene; but I'm not the queen
And still waiting for the perfect part in a day dream
To wear my prom dress to dance to the love story
But want another spot light for you on my stage
Every doors said "I don't know" but introduced sidekicks,
Pretending ' I'm alright' on the stairs with felicitated walk
And left my crown inside the cage for you to wear
So I'll leave; when screen closes with splendid end for you.

34. MOON ON THE GLOOMY SKY

Sometimes when my autumn dry leaves cracks
Held me to rise again on my own, strong bark, green tree
When the light flickers, the glass guarded when the flame was almost to die
Now this tired face, wet eyes has a shoulder for the cry and heart to trust
Never had any hold to cling on and to face my fear not alone
Support to my creepers; mother swan to the cygnet
Pillar to grow and refuge to the innocent for the world
Never letting go the moon, from the night gloomy sky,

35. REWRITING THE BEAUTY

The music plays loud on the background but I didn't dance
A million thoughts were coming by but I didn't write
It was the moment I knew I was lost and forgot I existed.
And why eyes are wet and my heart beat is rising
While your beautiful eyes look at me and my hands shivering
The air around me suddenly froze but I still can hear you.
Each and everytime my eyes reveals the truth from my heart
But I pulled it back so you won't get hurt, and I took it to myself.
I couldn't really resist the glow but I can stay far if you want me to
I could write a million songs every second of my life
But every single time I fail when your eyes sees me
Because no one could never find a better lyrics than your eyes
I'm fine with the reality but you know sometimes I lie.
And I want to rewrite the definition of beauty
With the mildest touch of the heart of yours
The nicest clouds were cold and the sun was burning
They were not a big wonder than you in front of me
While every eyes looked above mine were looking on to my beautiful

How can I write about the sky or the flower when my world is in front of me?

36. REPUTATION

Im the on a never ending road, but I know where it destined to
No one can see me and that doesn't matter unless you didn't bother
Still the eyes had never seen me driving with the ghost of you
Leaving the city and blaming the lights, remembering the hopeless smile.
I don't know the point or the plot of your eyes on me
Because this heart doesn't remember any clue that you gave
Maybe the dark lights on me, gleams when you look into my eyes
Gave a heart attack, blinding all the keys which was kept on your car
And I've got that attitude but it sometime it fails infront of you
Holding your reputation on my hand and you on other.

37. TEDDY

Sometimes words aren't enough to saythings
When it comes, its not much unsophisticated to express
It's all a sagacious heart to show
Still you gave the feel of love and secure
Without saying a single word you won
It was no solicited but all by love
To the one where I get teddy hugs and kisses.

38. ONE MOMENT

Sometimes it's all just a moment
Where the heart goes far away
Over the mountains across the sea
To read the scarlet letter of the dusk.
Where it says to imagine the place
Where you've been with the dandelion
Singing the gladdest don't for a while.
The solitary flickers as her eyelids did
Its all just a moment to know.
The stars will show up, glitters in the sky
The brightest star each and every eye seeks
But the tiniest is far higher than the brightest
Never been so funny all above high;
Its all just a moment to realise.
The scarlet becomes blue with the lying lie
While the sun closes it's eyes
She again showed up no hope
Just again the eyes flickered
The glimpsing smiling moon shines her
Tears in the cheek;
Its all just a moment to see.

39. IDYLLIC POETRY

The mirror pulled me to the reflection of you in it
My eyes smiled like never before skipping a heart beat.
When my bruised finger ran to touch the poised face
And quickly disappeared when the sun hit the tiny stars
Now I see you everywhere my feet goes
But the sudden realization, that you're not mine.
Came up like moon, on a sunny day out of nowhere
Was hard to believe, but darling; we are poetry
And nothing stopped me writing us, even there was no clue
The heat of the sun touched my cheek, and I felt you
Your ethereal and Idyllic eyes is a spark to the papers of my book
And they are burning bright every where I go
Reading all the pages again and again, untill they die
So I'll leave them to you when the moon goes down.

40. ASHES ALONG THE SHORE

The glasses pieces pierced my chest and tore the heart
My ribs and bones crushed and flying as butterflies, in the air
It's all over when you look up onto the sky, with your eyes open
The clouds that we share will bring the butterflies to you,
Save it with you because it was born from the guitar of my bleeding fingers
It'll wake you up every morning, with a kiss on your face
When you realize, the sky will not there to know me
And the trees will be withered to ashes along the shore

41. I WISH

A million words on my mind flying like it never been
Trying to catch them and wove then like a poetry and wear as a scarf
So it warms me up on a cold day of december.
Why all my loudest words I speak on my eyes,
And the silent speech I give when my mouth laugh
Can't be a teddy I hold everytime or lie on her lap;
While my heart beating the nightmares of my life.
A crowd with laughter and I'm a clown with a crown;
Where did my smile went after?
Did they go behind the clouds to bring happiness for me?
But I never seen the same clouds that I saw yesterday.
I wish my mirror could speak, and pillow could hug,
And my pen could hold, pages could give hope
And the stars could cry and breeze could whisper
For all the speech I give them, all night and every winter.
Torn heart embracing the beauty flaws,
Now I'm on a journey to find me and save me.
I want silent daydream than brightest nightmares
I don't hear with words, but with broken piece of my heart
I don't see with my eyes, but with poetry
So I wish I could turn deaf and blind and feel me.

42. WHAT DO YOU WANT ME TO DO

Its been years since I knew the perfume smell of your t shirt
I still cannot forget this star dust in this deep woods.
Searching them everywhere I go
The tears of agony couldn't make it's intentions on me.
Singing down the streets and stars on our eyes,
For the selfish desire that is weaved in my heart.
I scream "I don't want you just to see my smile
And I've got nothing, but the words and my broken heart
I know what you'll say when poems reach you again,
So what you want me to do?
Go to the cliff again?
Or to the peaks I've never been? "

43. TAKE MY RAIN BACK

The wolves chasing and my heart is pacing,
The thorns pierced my feet, but I kept running
I lost my breath in the middle of the race
I fell from the cliff not knowing where it takes
My hair pointing the heaven pleasing to take me,
But the ground pulled me down
My spine broke into pieces and I couldn't stand
But I found no wounds on my skin nor my smile was lost.
Heart is bleeding but my face is fine
I saw the pages of my story falling from sky
Even the heavens didn't like the ruined story
They were written these many years to just blew away
Cause I never knew how to handle the night sky
The cameras flashed in front of me, blinding my eyes
Not for my survival but to laugh at the plot
So wanting the sky to take my rain back.

44. REMEMBER

I know I cannot rewrite the stars and take them to home
But will you leave me to stare the moon on a cold rainy night?
Dreaming about the sky on the ground; and walk among them
Now I'm writing the letters again and again which I never post,
But I believe the night sky showed the sun into millions pieces of it
And I hope you open you windows to look at them, singing to the moon
While the leaves dancing to my breeze of songs I write everyday.
As my hands were not enough to hold them
I sent it to the sky, so when you look at them,
Remember;
They were the songs I left on the sky for you.

45. IM NOTHING

My voice is not clear as water like her
I'm not a daydream, which makes the sky pink and purple
But you know this 'once in a life time' made to forget the sky is so high
My world don't know how I see the skies and night
And it don't know how my eyes burn flawlessly, only when I see you
These flowers got no idea how my words bleed through my heart
I've lost my home with the scars of you on my face
Following the stars with a passion reaching them
I'm not a gold wrapped diamond ring
I'm not the million stars but a simplest rain drop
Im nothing;
I'm just a barren tree with paper and pen, with you as my inspiration;
But armed with love.

46. LEFT OUT

The need of the hour is to go to the peak and cry
I save every tears to talk with the night sky
Pretty cruel words pierced the air to give the thorn crown
The light is flickering, giving the sign for the end of the day.

I still remember when the champagne bottle broke
For me to to leave at the midnight, for the cheers
The pages have turned; the rose has drowned
But no one heard the call when the wind howled.

The only companion was the moon, not the light
Have you ever seen the dark side of the smile?
The fire buring on my skin shrank my heart,
But now blaming me for the thorns and scars I got.

Where will I go? To the silent sky to balter?
Or to the cliff, for me to go more further?
As I'm not the early spring to be adored for the answers,
Nor anything in the world that can be seen;
But the questions on the mind, after reading the story
That one thread from every scarf, which is pulled out
And that one book, which is always lefft out

47. BROKEN WINGS

Credulous path taking me far away
Simple was the character of the clock ticking for me
But the cynical counts gave by them was following
The roses that they pasted on the wall for the people
But none can see the rose thorns pricking which I've kept in secret,
And they never made me to leave the garden as that was my honor.

Without the crown and without the throne it gave the feeling
But nothing came to rescue nor the rain came to clean my hands
My mind is wandering in the winter night, wishing the lights will lead
To the right and wrong , pleasing to show the way
They wandered again until they see the paradise.
And you are not where you used to be
So the butterflies flapped their broken wings to seek.

48. NOT MINE

Drizzle on my cheek feel like a snow
The clouds are dripping the love every day,
For me to write a poetry for you under the dark clouds.
And smile to myself, watching you grow like fine wine
But I kept on writing, on ocean tides and still hoping.
Not for the flowers to bloom to create a spring morning
But the dandelions to fly away as a unfulfilled wish;
Just moving along the sky to rain for the roses.
The silence under my feet eroding; but the love echoing
The trees were sleeping while my wisteria is lost,
As there was a path leading to the clouds
And my diamond ring has lost in the river of beauty
It is in the fingers of delight that I don't deserve to stay.
That didn't hurt, but knowledge of you did
Holding on to the thoughts is not mine;
Never mine.

49. WAYFARER

I don't want to go with this excruciating love and lost in the way
Because I'm a wayfarer with broken wings and lost crown;
Solivagant journey under the presence of dark clouds
Making everything I see to go in vain and bringing back the night
And I saw all my thoughts wandering endlessly,
Scattered like my heart with a desire of making it right.

These broken pieces are not a mosaic on my canvas
Still helping and trying to fix the mess with stardust.
But where will I go when I'm caged behind the dark clouds of mine
So I wanted to go home, but what it seems is never was.
Somewhere in my heart is aware that I belong to the sky
As only the fantasies of the sky, makes flowers to bloom
And I don't wanna lose anything for you
But I slipped again, along with ocean current and lost my breath this time.

50. BROKEN SWORD

I've got all the scars on my face, leading me to the darkest places
The sun is burning them even when I hide
Where can I go when I'm forbidden to this entire world
I couldn't enjoy the day light while the strom ruling me inside
All my broken pieces was never together fro when I was stoned.
Left me all alone with a ache of love inside me
But the ropes tieing me down, never let me go anywhere
Do I have to wait till spring, to bloom my heart
To wipe my blood tears and clean my weary face?
But I've never seen them from the beginning
Why they didn't show up?
Are they waiting for my sword to break?

51. GIVE ME THE REASONS

I heard all the noises which I never have to hear
But those voices blocked all the doors which was kept for me
Forgetting all the prizes and threw it into the river.
The salt air burning the wounds I got everyday
Each and every breeze is not a zephyr on the spring
Everything is fading like the rainbow on a sunny day
I walked away for the sake of goodness
I want nothing in return but this life has got something
Which is not the light, but the moon's reflection on the lake
You drown to feel the salient touch of the nights beauty.
I left the place with my eloquent note on the gate
But no one knows it, even when years turn it
So I'm leaving but the sky looked at me the same way
It killed me the same, when the roses started to bloom
Now it is laughing at the scars on my body
Some were made but I drew some on my heart
And made it to bleed to make it as a plot of the flim.
Dieing to keep it but I left it to heal the hoax
It's scarier when cuts of the knife on my skin was bleeding again
No one will believe when they say the moon is under the ocean

So as they saw my scars with the eyes of wondering it is not
What made it you to see it as the pretending traitor,
Give me the reasons how your heart turned blind to see what is not.
I drowned but I felt the moon under my barren feet
So now some heart can now believe when you feel.

52. SILENT KISS AND LAVENDER SMILE

You make every flower bloom when they about to die
The wind that rushed through my hair gave a serenity on my cheek
Saying that this is how the light floats on the ocean
Like the eyes of thine speaks millions of unwritten letters
Giving a glimpse every singles time when reach the sight of mine
I saw the Auroras between the prose I write
Never knew the warmth along the stairs but now
Gave me those roses under the daylight
While your eyes whispering the loudest song to me
I felt the cold water from the sky and gave me everything
I'm not afraid of the crowd anymore
As now I know the purpose of stars on the night sky
But my moon gives me the silent kiss at every sight
And a lavender smile at every dawn

53. ECHO OF HAPPNIESS

All those tiny eyes aching for a true love to see
Like a billion stars in the sky, you can count the whole when you really feel
Flowers on our parallel way depicting the realization of truth
Hearing all the thorns in my heart and made me to go a mile with a cure.
As an innocent hand run for a hoping finger of her mother,
Without of her knowledge for a feel of safe and secure
So goes my mind to you, for a smile on my face
For a sound mind to hear the echo of happiness.

54. ENDLESS EPIPHANY

These goes my heart to you like waves reach the shore
Singing the song, while I see myself in your enchanting eyes
To and fro endlessly with a hope of seeing you again
But this clueless heart was not able to find a reason of your rain.
The moments with you always reflectiing the shine on my face
While my heart overflowing with love as there is no space
Healing all my hurts and giving a zephy of happiness
And I'm not perfect to witness those smiling gaze of yours.
I never found any love when I'm with those special eyes
But I could feel the poetry talking to my heart endnessly
Have you ever listened to my secret silent of my eyes?
It always speaks the brilliant light of your symphony smile.
Even the sun may smite the world with darkness
But my hands will always hold you till the very end.

55. HIM

In the dark I saw the light
My heart beat raised at my first sight
I kept my eyes open when would see me
My eyelashes have'nt closed cause in you I wanna be
I'm not able to see your eyes when you
But my vision always sees more than the few
Tears flows not that I couldnt get you
But because; I don't wanna miss you.

56. SADDEST STORY

Living in a small world of a tremendous place
Where everyone said there's no space
Suviving with full of suffocation
There she saw an inspiring creation.
She gave her talent with her whole heart
But the light considered not even a dot
She was left in the deep blue sea
Where she found no people to be;
She felt the same suffocation there
The voices outside, she could hear
Still she was left in the deep blue
Where that none gave a clue
The tears on her eyes flowed like an river
No one cared as she already in the ocean mere.
"The world's best" in the story of thine
Is the worlds saddest story of mine.

57. ONE LAST TIME

The night sky and cold rain was testing me
But now every single breath is tempting
Sending the farewell letter to the dusk
A small light far away, flickering a good bye to me
A smile raised my lips, with a glance of fragrance
Little shine glowed on the corner of my eye.

Chose bare foot, just to feel the wet sand;
Flashback to the summer that will never come back
The story is reaching the shore without the hero's entry;
Writing the last line of the book but I wish it had a better ending
The plot was so strong, it needed many hearts to continue.

You never knew the beginning nor the journey
Where you were the sun to the garden
Now I wish atleast you'll memorize the last line.
You said that the skies are painted with love letters
I had to give my last tear to complete the brightest picture

I wish we never met;
I wish that the horizon was never existed

As it is hard to erase the colours flashing in my eyes
Rendering in my heart, but now I had to give it back
One last grey cloud above the ocean
Promise it's the last, as I don't wish to kill with choice I have.

9 798887 491431

Printed by Libri Plureos GmbH in Hamburg,
Germany